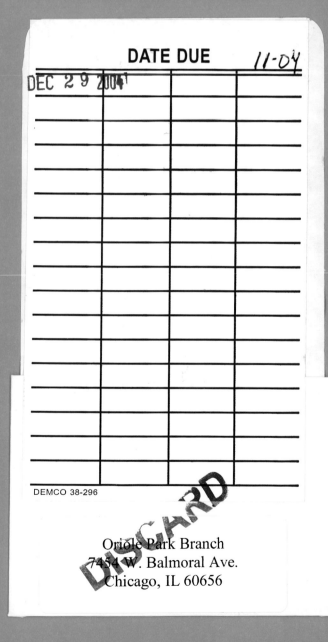

DATE DUE   11-04

DEC 2 9 2004

DEMCO 38-296

Seurat
and
La Grande Jatte
CONNECTING THE DOTS

by Robert Burleigh

Published in association with The Art Institute of Chicago

HARRY N. ABRAMS, INC., PUBLISHERS

Can a painting tell a story, if you look at it long enough?

Perhaps a painting can tell many stories. Or perhaps it can begin stories—leaving it to us to wonder about the endings. One thing, though, is certain. There is a famous painting that can tell the story of what life was like in a park on a Sunday afternoon long ago. It can also tell the story of the man who painted it—Georges Seurat (pronounced *Zhorzh Sirrah*) and how he viewed his world. It can even tell us what Georges thought about the art of painting itself!

The only known photograph of Georges Seurat, date and photographer unknown

A Sunday on La Grande Jatte—1884, 1884–86, oil on canvas, 88⅝ x 133⅞ inches

The title of the painting is *A Sunday on La Grande Jatte—1884.* Let's stop, look closely, and see what *La Grande Jatte* has to tell us.

What do we notice first?

How about this? *La Grande Jatte* is huge—around seven feet high and ten feet wide! You might say that it doesn't just hang on a wall. It completely covers a good-sized wall. And if the painting itself is big, so is the scene it shows. Take a look. Around fifty people—count them if you can!—as well as three dogs and a monkey, are scattered in and around an island park near Paris, France. The park is called La Grande Jatte. (In French, that means "the large jar," so named because of the island's shape.) La Grande Jatte lies in the Seine, the famous river that cuts Paris into two halves. It is a sunny Sunday in 1884, over 100 years ago. This was a time when most people worked six long days a week and were quite happy to have Sunday off. So—for some Parisians at least—Sunday was a day to escape from the heat of the city

The park, La Grande Jatte, as it appeared in 1999. This photograph shows a view similar to the painting.

In 1985, Robert Sivard made this picture that he called *Imaginary Painting of Georges Seurat in His Studio* (medium and size unknown). The work reveals how large Seurat's painting is and suggests how the artist may have created it.

and head for the shade of trees and the cool breezes off the river. And at first glance, that's what we see: many different people, relaxing in a park by the river. What are they doing?

On the right, a fashionable couple (that's the woman with her sunshade and the man in his top hat) is on a promenade, or stroll. Across the way, another woman—also well dressed—extends her fishing pole over the water. But that's only a start.

How many of the following people, animals,
and objects can you find?

- A monkey on a leash.

- A strangely small man with a black hat and thin cane, looking at the river.

- A white dog with a brown head. (A clue: it's far in the distance.)

- A woman knitting.

- A man playing a horn.

- Two soldiers standing at attention as the musician plays.

- An old woman hunched under an orange umbrella.

- A man with a pipe.

- A woman under a parasol in a boat filled with rowers.

- A couple admiring their infant child.

- A tiny pink butterfly. (Another clue: it's up close but not easy to see.)

- A few pieces of white paper that seem to be littering the otherwise clean stretch of grass.

How many did you find? All of them? Good for you.

But we could go on and on and on, because Georges Seurat filled his park scene with so many people! And perhaps he was having fun with some of them, too.

Look at the big, black dog—
is he munching on someone's picnic?

And what about the young woman holding a bouquet of flowers? Do you think she will give the bouquet to a friend this afternoon?

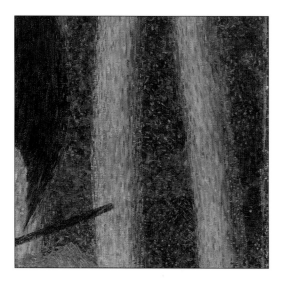

Here is one detail that you probably *didn't* see. Almost completely hidden among the trees, in the upper right of the painting, a figure is lurking. Who he or she is we don't know. In fact, you have to look hard at the actual painting to see that someone is there!

The mystery begins. We think we're looking at a typical Sunday in Paris, 1884. But is this really so?

Yes—and no. Look again! The large crowd doesn't seem to be moving! It feels odd, as if time has suddenly—stopped!

Turn back to the couple on the right: the woman wearing a strange, bell-shaped skirt and the man with his walking stick and cigar. Are they talking? No. They aren't even looking at each other! Both of them stare straight ahead, almost as if the other person isn't there.

And what about those figures on the left, seated or leaning back in the grass? The two men seem to be thinking their own thoughts, not noticing each other—or anyone else. Each is quite lost in his own private world.

Or look at the woman in the painting's center, with the small child in white. How motionless they are, as if waiting for a camera's shutter to snap!

A strange stillness. An almost eerie silence. A sense of mystery. Feelings like these hover over the entire painting, do they not? Nearly everyone appears to be quite alone. Alone. Quiet. Absorbed by something—but what that something is we can't tell. True, the little girl in the orange dress

is running—but even she looks frozen in midair. The trees themselves stand like silent sentinels, or guards, in the island landscape.

Let's think about this. Maybe Georges wasn't interested in only showing people relaxing outdoors on a sunny afternoon. Maybe he wasn't trying to present a typical day in a park.

Instead, maybe he wanted to freeze a single moment in time. Have you ever wished you could stop the clock—bingo!—just like that?

You would be able to see everything exactly as it is right now: the way your friends dress, the places they go to have fun, the games they play. You could point at things around you and say to people, "See, this is the world I live in. How does it look to you?"

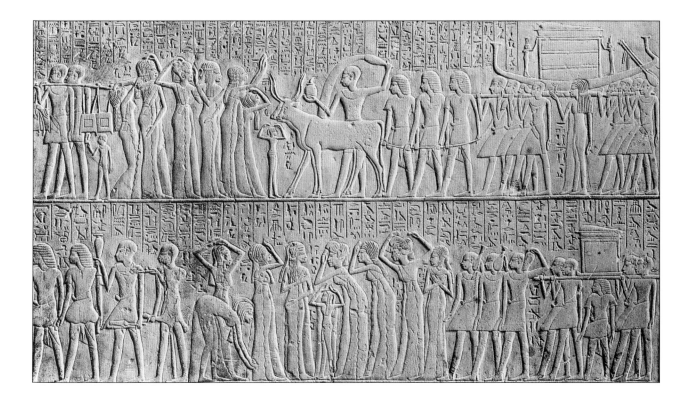

This Egyptian tomb fragment showing a processional is similar to the ancient work that inspired Seurat.

Perhaps that's why the figures in *La Grande Jatte* are so statuelike. We can imagine Georges saying: *Here is a park on a Sunday in 1884. Let me show it to you in a way that you will remember it—for all the years to come!*

Once, walking with some friends, Georges passed an ancient sculpture of people in a slow-moving line, or procession. He looked at the carved figures. Then he announced: "Someday I want to make a picture where modern people file by, just like that." Is *La Grande Jatte*, perhaps, the result of this wish? Many over the years have thought so.

Something else about *La Grande Jatte* is unusual.

Look at the surface of the painting. Do you see how the paint has been put on? Do you see them—the many hundreds of them? Yes, the dots!

From a distance, each large area of the painting (the light- or dark-green grass, say, or the purple of the woman's skirt) appears to be a single color. But come closer—and even closer! There, you see—dot, dot, dot. *La Grande Jatte* is covered with tiny dots, which are really small brush-tips of paint. And these dots—rather than lines or broad, flat sweeps of color—make up the people, the grass, the water, the trees. Think of the artist working slowly, covering a seven-by-ten-foot canvas—seventy square feet—with dots! It must have been very hard and taken him a long time.

Why did Georges decide to work this way?

Think how light dazzles and sparkles on a sunny day. Sometimes it is so strong you have to blink or rub your eyes. That's a bit like what's happening here. The dots help us to see light bouncing off objects.

Keep on looking. Is it your darting eyes or is it the dots themselves that make the colors seem to dance? True, the people in the painting may not be moving, but the dots seem to be! This vibrating color makes the surface of the painting more interesting, more lively, more fun to gaze at and to try to figure out. Yes, it takes more time to see everything Georges put into his composition. But maybe he wanted us to slow down and really look!

The dots are one of the elements that make *La Grande Jatte* so special.

Above: Seurat's trees stand like the columns in this drawing of an ancient Greek building. Right: *Tree Trunks,* 1884, conté crayon on paper, 18⅝ x 24½ inches

Georges was a careful painter. He thought about

many things in composing his painting. "Art is harmony," he once remarked. He explained that harmony comes about when an artist is able to balance shapes and colors so that all the parts of a painting work together.

Let's look for some of the shapes in *La Grande Jatte.* Look at the tree trunks, standing like columns throughout the picture. And notice some of the people, like the large couple on the right, or the woman with an umbrella standing in the center, or the fishing woman on the far left. They, too, seem to hold up the painting from within because they are so straight and tall.

These vertical forms are balanced by quite different ones. Do you see the curved shapes, like small hills, that the tops of the parasols make? How many parasols (not counting the ones in the far distance) can you count? If you found five, you're right. Starting with the woman by the riverbank on the left, five parasols with their round tops are placed across the composition, repeating themselves one after the other—like a line all the way across the painting.

An example of a parasol

The dark shadows on the grass seem to move, not up and down, but from left to right. The large shadow closest to us does this. And so do the many smaller shadows farther back. Do you see their thin shapes getting smaller and smaller the farther from us they are? They, along with the figures, which also grow smaller, help draw our gaze back into the distance. . . .

So what do we have? A picture as big as a wall. More than fifty people. Hundreds and hundreds of dots. By now you're probably asking: How long did it take Georges to finish this very complicated painting?

Well, listen to this:
It took him over a year.

Above: *The Chariot Race,*1876, by Jean-Léon Gérôme (oil on panel, 34 x 61½ inches), shows the traditional style typical of the work popular during Seurat's lifetime. Facing page: These paintings were made by artists who abandoned tradition and became known as the Impressionists.

Some artists, it's true, get an idea and paint their pictures quickly. A group of artists in France at the same time as Seurat were called Impressionists. They frequently painted outdoors, where they made impressions, or quick sketches, of the scenes in front of them. They were interested in views of modern life, rather than in old-fashioned subjects based on mythology or history.

Georges admired and learned from the Impressionists. But he himself was a different kind of artist. He thought for a long time about what he wanted to paint. One friend summed up his way of working by saying, "Georges never did anything on impulse," which is to say that he never did anything without thinking about it first!

Top: *The Artist's House at Argenteuil*, 1873, by Claude Monet, oil on canvas, 23¹¹⁄₁₆ x 28⅞ inches; bottom left: *Acrobats at the Cirque Fernando*, 1879, by Pierre Auguste Renoir, oil on canvas, 51¾ x 39⅛ inches; bottom right: *Woman and Child at the Well*, 1882, by Camille Pissarro, oil on canvas, 32 x 26⅛ inches

Georges was very interested in colors.

He paid attention to how they can help create different feelings. Did you ever wonder why some colors make us feel sad while others make us feel happy? Cozy and warm? Lonely and cold? He spent many hours thinking and reading as he tried to answer these questions.

Georges noticed how certain colors, placed side by side, make one color "stand out," or appear stronger. For example, the many blue dots in *La Grande Jatte*'s dark, shaded areas, placed next to the many orange dots in the light areas, look bluer—and the orange dots look even more orange! Or look at the narrow dotted border that runs completely around the painting. Do you see how the border's colors vary? That's because Georges wanted each section of the border to contrast with, or bring out, the colors beside it.

Georges worked slowly, almost more like a scientist than an artist. But he never forgot his ambition to be a great painter,

Landscape, Island of La Grande Jatte, 1884, conté crayon on paper, 16¼ x 24¾ inches

a painter whose work was not like anything that came before him. "I painted the way I did," he said, "because I wanted something new. I wanted a kind of painting that was my own."

How did Georges begin working toward *La Grande Jatte?* For one thing, he made a study of the park that was completely empty except for the trees and the shadows on the grass! And, one by one, he began imagining the people and animals he wanted to put into this space. Have you ever played with a felt board and arranged shapes on it? Georges approached his painting like that.

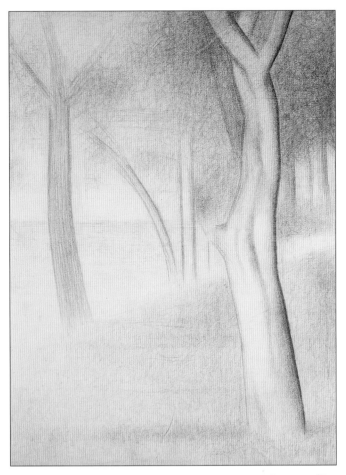

Left: *Trees*, 1884, conté crayon on paper, 24½ x 18⅝ inches; right: *Woman with a Monkey*, 1884, oil on wood, 9¾ x 6¼ inches

Some of his studies for *La Grande Jatte* are little paintings, which he did on the tops of cigar boxes! (Georges made up a word for these small works. He called them *croquetons*, which means "little sketches.") Other studies are drawings he made by rubbing a special black crayon over very rough, white paper. The crayon's soft black would catch on the raised parts of the paper; but the spaces between the raised parts remained untouched, and therefore white. Over the years, Georges did many of these dark/light drawings—often of working people, street scenes, or landscapes. Today, these studies are treasured for their simplicity and beauty.

Sometimes, Georges went to La Grande Jatte and drew what he saw there. At other times, he remained in his studio, on the seventh floor of a building in Paris. The room was cold in winter and hot in summer, and so tiny that when Georges was working on his final, large version of *La Grande Jatte*, he was unable to step back far enough to get a good look at it!

Standing Man, 1884, oil on wood, 6 x 9¾ inches

All the while, he still lived at home. His father supported him by giving him a small monthly allowance. His mother, for her part, prepared his dinner each night, to which Georges always arrived well dressed—even to the point of sometimes wearing a top hat.

Indeed, he was known for his businessman-like appearance. One fellow artist jokingly called him "the notary." (A notary is an official who signs important documents with a stamp.)

A few *La Grande Jatte* drawings—like the one of the woman fishing—seem to have been made rather quickly and easily. Others, though, were harder for Georges to get right. For example, he did a number of drawings of monkeys before he was ready to paint the animal. He visited the zoo to study monkeys, but in fact none of the drawings we have today show the monkey in the exact way

it looks in the final painting. In all, we know of more than twenty-five drawings and almost thirty smaller paintings that the artist made before starting *La Grande Jatte*. Certainly, there were more that he did not keep or that have been lost.

Georges also returned to the painting—even after he declared it "finished." He added more dots, especially orange and

Seven Monkeys, 1884, conté crayon on paper, 11¾ x 9¼ inches

yellow ones in sunlit areas to make the picture look more brilliant. If you look carefully, you can even see where he changed the clothing of the woman holding the monkey's leash, adding dots to give her skirt a more rounded look.

And then—*voilà,*
as the French say. There it was!

When *La Grande Jatte* was first shown to the public—in 1886—
it immediately attracted attention. And why not? First, there was its enormous size. Next, the huge cast of "posed" characters. Then, the strangely staring faces. And finally the dots, which made the bright colors blend and vibrate. Soon, Georges's dot style was given a name, pointillism. The French word *point* means—that's right—point or dot. *La Grande Jatte* was more luminous then than it is today. That's because a few of its brighter colors have darkened over time.

One art writer, looking at *La Grande Jatte*, called it the beginning of an important new style: Neo- (or New) Impressionism. Another viewer noted

The catalogue cover from Seurat's first showing of *La Grande Jatte*

the careful, almost machinelike way Georges had applied the dots. He called the artist a "scientific" Impressionist. Still others compared *La Grande Jatte*, with its statuelike people, to ancient sculptures. One reviewer admired the painting because he felt Georges was poking fun at some of his stuffy fellow citizens. But not every observer was impressed. An unfriendly writer complained that the painting was nothing more than "cookie-cutter forms"!

Meanwhile, Georges, ever shy, quiet, and hardworking, just went on—working hard. (He even continued to work on *La Grande Jatte*. The dotted border was added later. He also built a white frame for his painting to better bring out its colors.) As usual, though, he talked little about his art. So why did he paint *La Grande Jatte?* We don't really know.

Evening, Honfleur, 1886, oil on canvas, 25¾ x 32 inches

During the next few years, he made many pictures using his newly invented dot style. In the summers, he visited the French coast. There, he painted seascapes in which the dots create lovely patterns of light and shadow. These pointillist scenes of harbors and the sea often express a deep quietness. One person said that Georges was the first painter to capture "the feeling the sea inspires on calm days."

In Paris Georges liked to wander among the evening crowds. He loved the brilliant effects of artificial lights. He was—as a friend put it—"haunted by night's magnificence." He drew and painted many scenes from nightclubs,

Circus, 1890–91, oil on canvas, 73¼ x 59½ inches

circuses, and street parades. Some of these later paintings were large, though none reached the size of *La Grande Jatte.*

What might he have done next? No one knows. Georges Seurat became very sick at age thirty-one—and died. The world had lost a great painter, though his art making had lasted only around ten years.

Time has passed. New art styles have come and gone. La Grande Jatte island is no longer a public park. But the painting that once took the park for its subject has lived on. *La Grande Jatte* stayed with Georges's family for several years. Today, however, it hangs in the Art Institute of Chicago, where viewers come to stand (or sit if they prefer, on a special bench provided for that purpose) before its mysteries. A picture made years ago by a then little-known artist is now one of the most well-known paintings in the world, celebrated in advertisements, songs, and stories.

Take one more look at Georges Seurat's most famous painting. It's fun to imagine that among the many people in the park—the musician, the soldiers, the pipe-smoker, the man sitting under a distant tree—the painter might be lurking here, too.

He's not, of course. But … his dots are here. His love of art is here. His spirit is here. So in a way, Georges is here—sitting just out of sight, perhaps behind a tree—somewhere inside his wonderful painting *A Sunday on La Grande Jatte—1884.*

Some Important Dates
in the Life of Georges Seurat

Drawing of
Georges Seurat by
Maximilien Luce,
1890

December 2, 1859 Georges Seurat is born in Paris, France.

1875   Attends his first drawing classes.

1876   Enters the famous École des Beaux-Arts (School of Fine Arts) in Paris.

1879–80   Enlists as a soldier in the French army.

1882   Rents a small painter's studio in a part of Paris where many other artists live.

1883   Shows his work publicly for the first time.

1884   Begins work on *La Grande Jatte*.

1886   Exhibits *La Grande Jatte* with the Impressionists in the spring.

1887   Meets artist Vincent van Gogh, who admires his paintings.

1887–91   Paints many pictures of the French seacoast and of Parisian life.

1889   Exhibits *La Grande Jatte* at an exhibition in Belgium, where it is praised by many artists.

March 29, 1891 Georges Seurat dies of diphtheria in Paris at the age of thirty-one.

Author's Note

Approaching Georges Seurat in a book for young readers presents a challenge. Not only was his life a tragically short one, it also lacked the romantic episodes that mark the lives of some other major artists: no mental instability, no trips to far-off places, no revolutionary political stands, no celebrated loves.

Fortunately, however, he created a number of wonderful paintings and drawings, and especially one painting that is among the most famous in the world: *A Sunday on La Grande Jatte—1884*. I have tried to view Seurat through the medium of this painting—its style, its subject matter, the manner of its making, and its reception during the artist's lifetime.

The book is not a biography. It includes details about Seurat's life, but mainly those that help the reader understand how Seurat thought, planned, and worked.

For, above all, Seurat was a working artist, extremely disciplined, always serious, and private to the point of secretiveness. (For example, the fact that he was the father of a young son was apparently unknown to both his friends and his parents until shortly before he died!) In focusing on *La Grande Jatte* and Seurat's relationship to it, I have excluded other biographical information. Seurat attended the École des Beaux-Arts in Paris, where he was a good but not outstanding student; he served briefly in the French army; he had artist friends and followers, including Paul Signac; and he knew some of the leading critics of his day—such as Félix Fénéon, who used the term "Neo-Impressionism" to describe Seurat's work.

But Seurat for the most part steered his own steady course. He wanted to be a painter who made a difference in the history of art—and with *La Grande Jatte,* he surely succeeded. Given his brief life, coupled with the continuing high interest in his work, he might be the perfect exemplar of the old saying "Vita brevis, ars longa." Life is short, art long.

Glossary

BORDER an edge that goes all around something.

COMPOSING another word for "making" that is often used when talking about music and art.

COMPOSITION a word for all of the different parts of the painting put together. The composition of *La Grande Jatte* includes the people and animals, the landscape, the river, the boats, and so on.

CONTRAST a difference between two very different colors or between light and dark. For instance, there is a big contrast between black and white.

CRAYON a stick of black or colored chalk or wax used for drawing

DETAIL a part of a picture.

ELEMENT a small part or detail of a larger whole.

FRAME a border, usually made of wood, that goes all the way around a painting. Frames help to protect paintings. They can be plain or very fancy.

HARMONY in music, a word for when different notes sound good together. Paintings that have colors that look good together also have harmony.

IMPRESSIONISTS a group of artists working in France in the nineteenth century who wanted to paint everyday life. Their paintings often have light, bright colors, and look like they were painted very quickly.

LANDSCAPE a type of painting that shows places like fields, forests, and mountains. Usually landscapes do not have many people in them.

Although depicting a similar scene to *La Grande Jatte, Bathing Place, Asnières,* 1883–84, (oil on canvas, 79 x 118 inches) predates Seurat's pointillist style.

LUMINOUS a word used to describe something that is bright and full of light. The moon is often called luminous.

NEO- (OR NEW) IMPRESSIONISTS a group of artists who worked after the Impressionists. The Neo-Impressionists also used bright colors, but their pictures often look more calm and still than paintings by the Impressionists.

PARASOL an umbrella used to keep off the sun.

POINTILLISM a style of painting using tiny dots or dashes of paint.

SCULPTURE a form of art that is carved or shaped by an artist, such as a statue.

SEASCAPE a type of painting that shows the ocean or the beach.

SHADE to darken; to add color.

STUDIO a place where an artist works and keeps all of his or her tools for making art.

STUDY a type of sketch or drawing that an artist makes to help plan for a larger work of art.

STYLE a certain way of making art. For instance, some artists with realistic styles make paintings that look real like photographs. Other artists use styles that make things look very different than they do in real life.

VERTICAL a word used to describe things that are upright. For instance, the trunk of a tree is vertical.

VIEW the point from which the artist seems to have been looking in order to depict a scene.

Selected Bibliography

Art Institute of Chicago Museum Studies, vol. 14, no. 2 (1989). A special issue devoted to *La Grande Jatte.*

Broude, Norma, ed. *Seurat in Perspective.* New York: Prentice-Hall, 1978.

Düchting, Hajo. *Georges Seurat 1859–1891: The Master of Pointillism.* Los Angeles: Taschen, 1999.

Herbert, Robert L. *Seurat: Drawings and Paintings.* Cambridge, Mass.: Yale University Press, 2001.

Rewald, John. *Seurat: A Biography.* New York: Harry N. Abrams, 1990.

———. *Seurat.* London: Thames and Hudson, 1965, 1997.

Acknowledgments

The author would like to acknowledge the help he received from Gloria Groom and Douglas Druick, the Art Institute of Chicago's curators in charge of the June 16–September 19, 2004, exhibition, *Seurat and the Making of "La Grande Jatte."* He would also like to thank the members of the Art Institute's publications department, particularly Susan F. Rossen, Amanda Freymann, Annie Feldmeier, and Katherine Reilly, for their advice and support on this project from beginning to end.

In *Chahut,* 1889–90 (above, oil on canvas, 66⅞ x 54¾ inches), and *Circus Sideshow (Parade de cirque),* 1887–88 (left, oil on canvas, 39¼ x 59 inches), Seurat continued to develop the pointillist style.

ILLUSTRATION CREDITS

Unless the caption states otherwise, all artwork is by Georges Seurat and all details are from *La Grande Jatte*. PAGE 2: Photograph of Georges Seurat. Courtesy of Robert L. Herbert, gift from Dr. Jean Sutter c. 1966. PAGE 3: Georges Seurat (French, 1859–1891). *A Sunday on La Grande Jatte—1884*, 1884–86. The Art Institute of Chicago, Helen Birch Bartlett Memorial Collection, 1926.224. PAGE 4: Photograph of La Grande Jatte. © Anthony Atkielski, 1999. PAGE 5: Robert Sivard (American, 1914–1991). *Imaginary Painting of Georges Seurat in His Studio*, 1985. PAGE 11: Egyptian tomb fragment. Courtesy of the Ryerson and Burnham Archives, The Art Institute of Chicago, from *Beschreibung der Aegyptischen Sammlung des Niederlandischen Reichsmuseums der Altertumer in Leiden* (Amsterdam, 1911), pl. 15. PAGE 14: Seurat. *Tree Trunks*, 1884. The Art Institute of Chicago, Helen Regenstein Collection, 1987.184; Columns. Courtesy of the Ryerson and Burnham Archives, The Art Institute of Chicago, from James Stuart, *The Antiques of Athens* (1794), vol. 3, ch. 9, pl. 2. PAGE 16: Jean-Léon Gérôme (French, 1824–1904). *The Chariot Race*, 1876. The Art Institute of Chicago, George F. Harding Collection, 1983.380. PAGE 17: Claude Monet (French, 1840–1926). *The Artist's House at Argenteuil*, 1873. The Art Institute of Chicago, Mr. and Mrs. Martin A. Ryerson Collection, 1933.1153; Pierre Auguste Renoir (French, 1841–1919). *Acrobats at the Cirque Fernando*, 1879. The Art Institute of Chicago, Potter Palmer Collection, 1922.440; Camille Pissarro (French, 1830–1903). *Woman and Child at the Well*, 1882. The Art Institute of Chicago, Potter Palmer Collection, 1922.436. PAGE 19: Seurat. *Landscape, Island of La Grande Jatte*, 1884. Trustees of the British Museum, London. PAGES 20–21: Seurat. *Trees*, 1884. The Art Institute of Chicago, Helen Regenstein Collection, 1966.184; Seurat. *Woman with a Monkey*, 1884. Smith College Museum of Art, Northampton, Massachusetts, purchased with the Tyron Fund, 1934; Seurat. *Standing Man*, 1884. The National Gallery, London. PAGES 22–23: Seurat. *Embroidery; The Artist's Mother*, 1882–83. The Metropolitan Museum of Art, New York, purchase, Joseph Pulitzer Bequest, 1951, acquired from The Museum of Modern Art, Lillie P. Bliss Collection. 55.21.1. Photograph ©1989 The Metropolitan Museum of Art; Seurat. *Woman Fishing*, 1884. The Metropolitan Museum of Art, purchase, Joseph Pulitzer Bequest, 1951, acquired from The Museum of Modern Art, Lillie P. Bliss Collection. Photograph ©1989 The Metropolitan Museum of Art; Seurat. *Seven Monkeys*, 1884. Musée du Louvre, Paris. © Réunion des Musées Nationaux/Art Resource, NY. Photograph: Michèle Bellot. PAGE 24: Catalogue cover. From Ruth Berson, *The New Painting: Impressionism, 1874–1886*, vol. 1 (San Francisco, 1996), p. 443. PAGE 25: Seurat. *Evening, Honfleur*, 1886. The Museum of Modern Art, New York, gift of Mrs. David M. Levy, 1957. Digital image © The Museum of Modern Art, New York. PAGE 26: Seurat. *Circus*, 1890–91. Musée d'Orsay, Paris, bequest of John Quinn, 1924. R.F. 2511. ©Réunion des Musées Nationaux/Art Resource, NY. PAGE 28: Maximilien Luce (French, 1858–1941). Drawing of Seurat. Courtesy of the Ryerson and Burnham Archives, The Art Institute of Chicago, from *Les Hommes d'aujourd'hui*, no. 368 (1890), cover. PAGE 30: Seurat. *Bathing Place, Asnières*, 1883–84. National Gallery, London. ©Erich Lessing/Art Resource, NY. PAGE 31: Seurat. *Chahut*, 1889–90. Kröller-Müller Museum, Otterlo; Seurat; *Circus Sideshow (Parade de cirque)*, 1887–88. The Metropolitan Museum of Art, New York, bequest of Stephen C. Clark, 1960. 61.101.17. Photograph ©1989 The Metropolitan Museum of Art. Many of the images in this book are protected by copyright and may not be available for further reproduction without the permission of the artist or other copyright holder.

To Ben Dallas and Jens Brasch —R. B.

Designer: Heather Zschock

Library of Congress Cataloging-in-Publication Data
Burleigh, Robert.
Seurat and La Grande Jatte : connecting the dots / by Robert Burleigh.
p. cm.
Summary: An analysis of Georges Seurat's famous painting, A Sunday on La Grande Jatte—1884, including where and when it was made, interesting details, and the techniques used to create a sense of stillness.
Includes bibliographical references and index.
ISBN 0-8109-4811-7
1. Seurat, Georges, 1859–1891. A Sunday on La Grande Jatte—1884—Juvenile literature. 2. Seurat, Georges, 1859–1891—Criticism and interpretation—Juvenile literature. [1. Seurat, Georges, 1859-1891. Grande Jatte. 2. Seurat, Georges, 1859–1891—Criticism and interpretation. 3. Art appreciation.] I. Title.

ND553.S5A68 2004
759.4—dc22
2003014256

Printed and bound in China
10 9 8 7 6 5 4 3 2 1

Harry N. Abrams, Inc.
100 Fifth Avenue
New York, NY 10011
www.abramsbooks.com

Abrams is a subsidiary of

LA MARTINIÈRE
GROUPE